THE SECRETS WE BURY

DINA CAHANEY

This book is lovingly dedicated to my family and friends, whose support and love have shaped me, and to the little town I grew up in, Carle Place, NY.
To the memories, the community, and the charm of a place that holds a special spot in my heart—though as for any buried secrets or bodies, if they exist, I know nothing about them.

One

Ash Mitchell didn't hear his alarm blaring through his headphones until his mom burst into the room, her face a blend of disappointment and frustration he'd seen a thousand times. He yanked the headphones off, swearing under his breath as she shook her head.

"It's your last chance, Ash. Don't screw this up," she said, her tone hovering somewhere between a plea and a warning.

Ash sat up, shrugged, and muttered, "Yeah, yeah, I got it." But he didn't have it—he'd never had it. Life wasn't something he had much control over; it felt like it was always controlling him, keeping him in the same dreary loop. A miserable job, the same arguments with his parents, the fights that left him more exhausted than any workday ever could.

He stumbled out of bed and into the bathroom, popping two muscle relaxers from the bottle he kept hidden under the sink. The warmth trickled over him, and for a few minutes, he could pretend everything was fine.

By the time he clocked in at the garage, the numbness had faded, but his temper simmered under the surface. Working on cars wasn't his passion, but it was the only job he'd managed to keep for a few months now. Mostly, he liked the people—well, he liked what they could offer him. Whether it was a few bucks he'd "borrowed" from coworkers or a smoke break he stretched to twenty minutes, he always managed to get what he wanted.

The hours crawled by, every task feeling like a monumental weight on his shoulders. Finally, toward the end of the day, just as he was ready to punch out, Ash heard his supervisor call his name. The tone was gruff, and Ash knew this wasn't just about a misplaced wrench or a late lunch break. He walked into the office, trying to appear casual, though his mind raced, trying to remember if he'd been careless.

His supervisor, a tall, burly man with oil-stained hands and a look that could drill through steel, looked down at Ash with barely concealed contempt.

"Ash, we're done," he said, voice flat. "You're fired."

Ash's heart sank, but he forced a smirk. "For what?" he asked, crossing his arms defiantly.

"Don't play dumb. We caught you on camera. You've been helping yourself to inventory, taking parts without paying." His supervisor leaned in, voice low. "I don't know what kind of game you think you're playing, but I've had enough."

Ash could feel the anger rising, a familiar heat building in his chest. He wanted to argue, to blame someone else, but he knew it wouldn't work. Not this time.

"You'll regret this," he muttered, grabbing his jacket and storming out of the office. On his way out, he ignored the glances from his coworkers, the whispers he could feel lingering in the air. He'd never admit it, but their judgment stung. It always stung.

He stomped into the parking lot, where he sat in his beat-up car, breathing heavily. His hands shook as he reached into his glove compartment, his fingers brushing the pill bottle that had become his only refuge. He twisted off the cap, downed a few more pills, and leaned back, letting the familiar numbness take over.

For a moment, he felt the weight lift, the suffocating pressure of expectations, guilt, failure. Everything faded, even his anger, even his father's voice nagging at the back of his mind, saying he'd never amount to anything, that he was wasting his life.

But deep down, Ash knew. This was just the *beginning*. His life was on a path, and it was headed somewhere dark.

Two

Ash sat at the corner of the dimly lit bar, nursing a beer while the jukebox played some scratchy tune in the background. The place was busy enough to feel alive but quiet enough for his thoughts to wander. He had been coming here for years, a sanctuary of sorts, where the world outside felt a little less demanding.

Ash raised an eyebrow as the bartender approached, carrying the bar's old rotary phone in one hand, the cord dragging behind her. The bartender set it down on the bar in front of Ash with a heavy thud.

"A call?" Ash frowned. "Here?" "Yeah, your sister or somethin'. Said it was important."

Ash's stomach tightened. He slid off the stool, leaving his beer behind, and followed the bartender's direction. The old rotary phone hung on the wall, its cord stretched taut from years of use. He picked it up, the cool plastic unfamiliar in his palm.

"What?" he grumbled, irritation lacing his tone.

There was a pause, then Chelsea's hesitant voice came through. "Hey, Ash... I, uh, I need a ride to volleyball practice. Mom and Dad are at work, and Anna's not around."

He rolled his eyes, pinching the bridge of his nose. "Why me? You know they don't want you asking me for favors."

She hesitated. "Yeah, I know. But I don't have a choice right now. I'll be late if you don't take me."

For a moment, he wanted to say no, to tell her to find someone else, anyone else. But something about her voice held him back. He knew Chelsea didn't call him because she wanted to—she called him because he was her only option. And that stung, though he wouldn't admit it.

"Fine. Where are you?" "Home," she said quietly. "Can you be here in ten?"

He didn't respond, just hung up, walked to his car and shoved the keys into the ignition. He was halfway back to the house before he wondered if he'd made a mistake. What if his parents found out? They'd probably lose it, lecture him about being irresponsible or embarrassing the family again. But something inside him—the same knot of curiosity, or maybe even pride—kept him from turning back.

When he pulled up to the curb, Chelsea was waiting out front, a duffel bag slung over her shoulder. She climbed in without a word, only giving him a quick nod before staring out the window.

He didn't know what to say, so he just started driving, the silence between them heavy and tense. A part of him wanted to ask why she hadn't just waited for Anna, or how practice was going, but he wasn't sure he wanted to hear the answers. He could tell by her stiff posture and the way she avoided looking at him that this was as awkward for her as it was for him. After a few minutes, she spoke, her voice barely above a whisper. "Thanks for coming."

"Yeah, whatever," he mumbled. He tapped his fingers against the steering wheel, glancing at her out of the corner of his eye. "Didn't think you'd actually call me."

"Neither did I," she admitted, finally looking his way. Her expression was unreadable. "But it's not like you're doing anything else, right?"

Her words hit harder than he expected, but he forced himself to chuckle, brushing it off. "Touché."

They drove in silence for a bit longer until the high school gym came into view. He pulled up to the curb, the engine idling as she gathered her things. She hesitated for a second, gripping the door handle, then turned to look at him.

"Look, I know you're... going through stuff," she said, her voice softer. "But maybe if you tried a little harder, things could be different. For you. For all of us."

He opened his mouth to respond, but the words wouldn't come. The raw honesty in her tone threw him off. He was used to arguments, to the bitterness that came from his parents. But not this—this felt like she still held onto some shred of hope for him, even when he had none left for himself.

"See you later, Ash," she said, and before he could answer, she stepped out and closed the door, leaving him alone with his thoughts.

As he watched her walk toward the gym, the weight of her words settled around him like a heavy blanket.

Three

Ash barely registered the world around him as he left the high school parking lot, the effects of the painkillers sinking in deeper with every passing mile. His mind drifted, hazy, and he struggled to keep his focus on the road. Home was the last place he wanted to go; the thought of his family's quiet stares and whispered judgments made him clench the steering wheel until his knuckles turned white.

Old Westbury was a place of mansions, lawns, and unspoken rules, and he'd been breaking them his whole life. He could feel the eyes of his parents' neighbors even when he was alone, like they could see right through the walls of their secluded, sprawling home. They knew who he was, what he'd done, and he could practically feel them all writing him off.

Instead, Ash pointed his car toward Hunter's Pub, the one place that didn't care who he was or what he did. The regulars here had their own share of messes and secrets, and it didn't matter if you were rich or broke, wasted or sober; they were just here to drink and forget. The place was dark, with a jukebox that croaked out old tunes, a pool table where a lucky few could swindle a few extra bucks, and a bartender who poured generously as long as the cash kept coming.

Ash parked and slid out, walking through the dim doorway into the familiar haze of stale beer and cigarette smoke. He didn't waste time, nodding at Martha, the bartender, who already had a shot of whiskey ready for him. "Need a second?" she asked, eyebrow cocked, her low-cut tank top and tattoos catching the eye of every guy who walked in. He barely looked at her, just downed the first shot and let her pour another.

The door swung open, and a burst of laughter caught his attention. Four people strolled in—a couple of rich kids dressed to the nines, two guys in designer clothes, and their girlfriends, who looked like they'd just come from a high-end club. The girls went straight to the jukebox, throwing on some pop song Ash didn't recognize, dancing and laughing loud enough to make the regulars stare. The guys looked around with a cocky grin, and their eyes settled on the pool table.

Ash smirked. Perfect. A couple of easy marks. He waved to Buck, a scruffy regular who he'd hustled pool with before, and swaggered over to the group. "How about a game? You two against us?" he said, eyes flicking from one guy to the other. They exchanged glances, their grins widening, clearly ready for a challenge.

The game started easy enough. The girls watched, still dancing to the beat of their song, barely paying attention as their boyfriends got into the game. But as the rounds went on, Ash could see the glint in their eyes, the competitiveness sparking. They were good, better than he'd expected, and each time they sank a shot, his frustration grew.

Near the end, one of the girls let out a loud whoop as her boyfriend made a tricky shot, and Ash's concentration snapped. His jaw clenched, and for a second, he imagined smashing the cue ball into the guy's face, the image so vivid it made his fingers itch. But he blinked, shaking himself, and forced his focus back to the game. They were down to the last few balls, and he was sure he'd make his shot—until he missed.

The rich kids laughed, celebrating as they shook his hand. Ash gritted his teeth, nodding stiffly before slipping out the back door to cool off. Outside, he took a shaky breath, pulling out a cigarette and lighting it, trying to calm himself. Anger pulsed through him, winding up in a tight coil in his chest that he needed to release.

He looked down at the nearly empty pill bottle in his hand and popped the last two painkillers. He knew he'd need more, and soon.

Just then, the rich kids walked out, laughing and chatting, the girls hanging on the guys' arms. They waved a lazy "goodnight" to him, and he gave a halfhearted shrug in response, watching as they sauntered past. He eyed their expensive clothes, the carefree way they held themselves, and a surge of bitterness welled up inside him. People like them had it all—money, stability, the kind of lives that would never be touched by someone like him.

Once they disappeared around the corner, he tossed his cigarette to the ground and went back inside, where Martha had another shot waiting for him. He smiled at her, though it didn't reach his eyes, and threw back the whiskey. She poured him another, smiling with that crooked, knowing look.

"Rough night?" she asked.

He nodded, taking the second shot and downing it, hoping it would drown out the mess swirling inside him.

Ash sat hunched over his drink, staring into the amber liquid as if it held the answers to questions he wasn't ready to ask. The low murmur of voices and the rhythmic clink of glasses filled the air, a soundtrack to his quiet escape.

The bartender appeared again, this time carrying the bar's old rotary phone in one hand, its coiled cord trailing behind. She set it down on the bar with a thud, right in front of Ash.

"It's for you," the bartender said, arms crossed. "Your mom." Ash glared at the phone like it was some unwelcome intruder. "You serious?" "Yeah. She's been calling nonstop. Figured you'd wanna get it over with," the bartender replied, giving him a pointed look before stepping away to pour someone else's drink.

Four

Ash woke to a pounding headache, the taste of stale whiskey coating his mouth like dust. He groaned, rolling over on his mattress, eyes cracking open just enough to take in the familiar mess of his room. Posters of old rock bands hung peeling from the walls, dishes with crusted leftovers littered the floor, and the sharp scent of something sour floated up to greet him. He reached blindly for the painkillers on his nightstand, but when his fingers brushed an empty bottle, reality crashed down like an unwelcome weight.

"Shit." He muttered, shaking the bottle as if it would miraculously refill. He tossed it aside, feeling his anxiety start to creep in. He needed a fix, something to get him through the day. The idea of sitting here with a splitting head and his own empty thoughts was unbearable.

The last thing he wanted was to bump into his parents, who were relentless in reminding him of his failings. It was the same routine every day: his dad demanding he find a steady job, his mom offering halfhearted encouragement, telling him he was wasting his life. They had pretty much stopped helping him financially. The house was all they provided—a roof over his head, nothing more. And it didn't come without a price; their disappointment and resentment were the currency. Downstairs was quiet, unusually so. Usually, by Saturday morning, his mom, June, would be curled up on the couch with one of her mystery novels, and his dad, Thomas, would be holed up in his office. But today, the silence stretched, thick and hollow, and it sent a strange chill down Ash's spine. He shoved the feeling aside, though, glad to avoid another clash with his father or a pitying look from his mother.

Ash filled a glass with water from the fridge and downed it in one go, feeling the coolness cut through his hangover, at least for a second. He put the glass down and started back up the stairs, eager to crawl back into his bed, pull the covers over his head, and shut out the world.

As he stumbled up the stairs, he noticed a dark mass on his bedroom floor. His black sweatshirt, soaked through, lay in a puddle of its own, the fabric clinging to the wood like it had been pulled from some swamp. It wasn't the kind of mess that would usually catch his eye, but something about it seemed... off. Water? Had he spilled something? He pushed the thought aside; whatever the explanation, he didn't have the energy to deal with it.

He fell into bed, pulling the covers up, burying himself in their worn warmth. The house remained eerily quiet, but instead of letting the discomfort creep in, he felt a twisted sense of relief. Finally, he didn't have to face June's tight-lipped frown or Thomas's sharp comments. There were no eyes watching him, no judgment pressing down on his shoulders.

As he drifted off, the questions that should have lingered—the wet sweatshirt, the silence, the empty house—faded into the background. For now, at least, he could escape.

Five

Ash was pulled from a fitful sleep by a loud knock at the door, the sound slicing through the quiet like a blade. Groggy, he rubbed his eyes, feeling the grit of sleep still clinging to them. For a moment, he lay still, trying to let the sound fade, hoping whoever it was would just give up and go away. The knocks turned to insistent rings of the doorbell, followed by more pounding on the door.

"Where the hell is everyone?" he muttered, pushing his pillow over his head to drown it out. But a stubborn curiosity got the best of him. Throwing his legs over the side of the bed, he shuffled to the window and peered outside. There she was, his mom's friend Stephanie, clicking back to her car in a huff.

Ash scowled. He had never liked Stephanie, his mom's overdressed friend with a superiority complex. A few months ago, he'd overheard her advising his mom to kick him out, saying that being coddled at home would only ruin him further. Stephanie's heels echoed off the driveway as she walked away, her hair swinging behind her with a kind of annoyance he found oddly satisfying.

Once her car pulled away, Ash trudged downstairs, more at ease in the silence. It was almost too quiet, though. Grabbing a bottle of water from the fridge, he downed it in one long gulp, then scanned the empty kitchen and living room, wondering again where everyone was. But with no one around to judge him, he figured this was as good a time as any to reach out to his dealer for a refill. He felt his pockets, finding nothing but lint and loose change.

He paused, a new plan forming. If no one was around, he could easily grab some cash from his parents' room. They'd never notice, and he'd pay them back eventually... or at least that's what he told himself. Creeping up the stairs, he felt a strange chill work its way up his spine as he reached his parents' bedroom door.

He pushed it open, and his breath caught in his throat.

There, in their bed, lay his parents, their bodies still, the sheets drenched in a horrific sea of blood. Ash's heart dropped, his stomach twisting as he staggered back, feeling the bile rise in his throat. He wanted to scream, but it was like his voice had left him. Everything felt like a nightmare, a surreal blur of terror and disbelief.

He clutched the doorframe, forcing himself to look away and catching his breath in short, desperate gasps. He didn't remember anything from the night before—no fights, no signs of trouble. But there was no denying what lay before him.

Stumbling back, he forced himself to turn toward his sisters' rooms. First, Anna's door. He could barely bring himself to open it, but something inside him needed to know. Inside, he found Anna sprawled in her bed, her face pale, her blonde hair matted with blood. The walls bore a dark splatter that froze him in place, as though the very room itself had died with her.

Panicked, he sprinted to Chelsea's room, flinging open the door. Empty. The relief was fleeting, swallowed quickly by the terror that gripped him tighter with every passing second. Where was Chelsea? Had she been here when it happened? Had she somehow escaped?

"What the... what the fuck?" The words slipped out, trembling on his breath as he tried to make sense of the horror before him. The fear crashed over him in waves, confusion swamping his thoughts. He pressed his hands to his temples, desperately trying to remember, to piece together any hint of what had happened.

Did he have something to do with this? His memory of the night before was a fractured haze, but surely he couldn't have done this... could he? The question gnawed at him, and as he stood there, the house around him began to feel foreign, hostile.

He forced himself back down the stairs, his mind racing. He knew one thing: he had to get out of there.

Six

Ash staggered into the living room, his mind reeling with thoughts he couldn't quite piece together. He went straight for the liquor cabinet, hands trembling as he fumbled with the door, grabbing a bottle of whiskey. His fingers gripped the glass neck as if it were a lifeline. He tipped the bottle back, the burning liquid hitting his throat with a force that nearly choked him. But he didn't stop, taking gulp after gulp, hoping the alcohol would somehow dull the shock or, better yet, spark some idea of what to do.

Setting the bottle down, Ash stumbled toward the bathroom, the room spinning around him. He gripped the sink, feeling the urge to retch but unable to. Instead, he leaned over, his breath coming in shallow gasps, and splashed cold water on his face, his hands trembling as he forced himself to look in the mirror.

The face staring back wasn't the Ash he remembered. His skin was pale, eyes bloodshot and hollowed with exhaustion. Beneath the mess, he caught a glimpse of himself as he used to be: a tall, handsome guy with dark hair that fell messily over his brow, contrasting sharply with his piercing hazel eyes. He used to turn heads, charm anyone he wanted, take whatever he desired. But whatever spark he'd had in his younger days was now buried beneath layers of recklessness, apathy, and anger.

He pulled away from the mirror, suddenly disgusted. Why was he the black sheep of this family? Why couldn't he be the model son like everyone else expected? And now, he was standing here wondering if he'd somehow killed them all in a drug-fueled blackout. The thought twisted in his mind, but he pushed it away with a sneer. His family's blood on his hands? He didn't think so.

Truthfully, he wasn't devastated that they were dead. No more judgment, no more nagging about jobs or responsibilities. But there was no way he could let this ruin his life. And there was still Chelsea to worry about. What if she came home and saw this? She'd be horrified, and she'd waste no time turning him in. Ash could practically hear her self-righteous voice tattling to the police, painting him as the family's resident screw-up.

He began pacing, the whiskey dulling his nerves but doing little to calm the storm in his mind. He needed a plan, something to cover his tracks or, at the very least, keep Chelsea from getting involved and ratting him out.

Just as he was about to head back upstairs to the scene he dreaded seeing again, the phone rang, its shrill sound slicing through the silence. He froze, staring at it as if it were some ominous message from the universe. His heart hammered as he walked toward it, unsure if he even wanted to answer. What if it was the police? Or worse... Chelsea?

Hands unsteady, he picked up the receiver, pressing it to his ear, and braced himself.

"Hello?"

Seven

Ash's heart thudded as he hung up the phone, already regretting ever answering. Stephanie's suspicion wasn't going to stop at a single call. She'd probably alert the police soon enough, and he had no idea how much time he had before someone showed up looking for answers. He forced himself to take a deep breath, steadying his hands as he rifled through his parents' room. His fingers closed around a wad of cash in his mother's drawer, and without a second thought, he shoved it into his pocket.

Without another look back, Ash left the house, practically stumbling out to his car. His mind was a fog of terror and desperation as he drove to the hardware store, his eyes darting to every car, every face, every glance that might linger too long. Pulling into the parking lot, he tugged a hat low over his face, hoping no one would recognize him.

Once inside, he went straight to the cleaning aisle, grabbing anything and everything he thought might help. Bleach, plastic sheeting, gloves, duct tape. He paused by the shovels and hesitated before tossing one into his cart. His stomach twisted as he piled the items in his arms and made his way to the register, his face set in stone as he tried to avoid the cashier's gaze.

But the young guy at the register was in no hurry. He moved at a painfully slow pace, his small talk grating on Ash's nerves. The whole time, Ash kept one eye on the window, half expecting a cop to walk in or someone he knew to spot him. When a police car rolled past outside, his pulse raced, and he shoved his cash at the cashier, barely waiting for change before bolting out to his car.

As he neared his house, his stomach dropped. A cop car was parked in front, and an officer was knocking on the door. Ash immediately pulled over down the street, gripping the steering wheel as he watched. The officer knocked again, peering in the window, but when no one answered, he eventually returned to his car and drove away. Ash waited until the police car was out of sight, then drove up to the house, his mind racing.

Back inside, Ash shut the door behind him, the silence pressing down like a weight. He dropped the bags on the floor and slumped against the door, his head swimming. He couldn't afford to hesitate now. He didn't know what he'd tell anyone who asked, what lie he'd come up with if someone pressed him, but he knew one thing: he had to cover his tracks, and he had to do it fast.

Eight

Ash leaned heavily against the liquor cabinet, taking long gulps straight from the whiskey bottle, letting the burn numb him. This was the only way he could prepare himself for the grim task ahead. His mind felt like it was unraveling, each thought twisted with regret and disgust, but he couldn't stop now. The dread in his stomach was relentless, weighing him down with each step as he dragged the plastic tarps into his parents' room, his movements automatic, his mind blank with horror.

The initial plan seemed simple in theory—wrap his parents in the tarps, drag them to the backyard, and bury them. But the fear gnawed at him, sharper with every passing second. If anyone found them, if anyone suspected him, it would all be over.

As he wrapped his father's still form, reality hit hard: dead weight was unforgiving. Every inch he tried to drag his father felt like hauling a mountain, and the thought of making multiple trips to the backyard was impossible. The whiskey in his veins wasn't strong enough to numb the weight of his actions, but it made him reckless, pushing him to the grim, unspeakable solution he'd been avoiding. He didn't let himself think about it for too long, because thinking would make him stop, and he couldn't afford that now.

He wrestled each of his parents into the master bathroom, bile rising in his throat as he forced himself to start the gruesome work. His stomach rebelled, and he barely made it to the sink before throwing up again and again, but he forced himself back. The hours dragged on as he hacked his way through the impossible, mind and body battling every step. Every sound seemed amplified—the drip of blood, his own ragged breaths, the nauseating scrape of tools. He emptied his mind of everything except the need to finish, forcing himself to ignore the horror of his own hands as he reduced the bodies to parts small enough to manage.

When he finally stuffed the remains into plastic bins, the heavy lids shut over the horror he'd created, he felt a flicker of hollow relief—just enough to stand up again. There was still so much to do. He scrubbed every inch of the bedroom, trying to erase every trace of blood. He stripped the bed, shoving the bloody sheets and blankets into the bins, only to realize with dread that the mattress itself was stained beyond hope. Gritting his teeth, he heaved the massive mattress over, struggling under its weight, forcing himself to forget the crimson soaking through the other side.

It was past midnight by the time he was done, his body aching, mind dazed with exhaustion and whiskey. The job wasn't clean or perfect, but it was done. He still had to face his sister's room, where Anna lay frozen in the same grim silence, but he pushed the thought away. He couldn't think about her, couldn't think about anything but getting these bins out of the house. He dragged each one through the darkened hallway, biting back the panic that threatened to overtake him as he realized how heavy they were. One by one, he pulled them into the backyard, the night thick with an eerie stillness that made his every movement feel like a shout.

The shed loomed in the shadows, empty, waiting. With a final heave, he shoved the bins inside, the lids sealing the horror away. He stood there, his chest heaving, his heart pounding as he shut the door, leaving everything inside in darkness.

Nine

Ash sat in his usual spot at the bar, his hands wrapped tightly around the cold glass, his mind hollow, emotions numb. It was strange, the way he could sit here, as if nothing had happened, as if he wasn't drenched in guilt, and horror hadn't become his shadow. The bartender poured him two shots, and Ash threw them back in quick succession, the burn barely registering. He kept his face impassive, feigning normalcy, as he struggled to keep his head from spinning back to what he'd done just hours before.

Every image flashed with painful clarity: Anna's small, lifeless body in his arms, the fresh earth he'd shoveled beside the oak tree, his mother's eyes vacant, his father's blood on his hands. The memories throbbed, filling his chest with something suffocating. And yet, as Ash sipped his beer, he forced himself to breathe, to sit still. He could feel the weight of his actions pressing down on him like iron chains, each breath a battle to keep it together.

Then the bar door swung open, and Ash's heart skipped. He glanced up, barely managing to control the flash of panic that crossed his face. Two men walked in, one dressed in a dark suit, the other in a casual jacket. The man in the suit, with an air of calm authority, walked straight toward Ash. Ash's stomach tightened as the man introduced himself in a low voice as Detective Harris. He gestured for Ash to come with them, explaining that they needed to ask him a few questions about his family.

"Your mom's friend Stephanie called in," Detective Harris explained, his tone sharp but neutral. "She's been trying to reach them for hours. Said it's been over a day without any contact, which is un-usual. And she's worried."

Ash forced a blank expression, nodding as if he was just as sur-prised by the news. He stumbled over a few mumbled words, some-thing about his family possibly going out, but he knew his excuses sounded thin. The detective studied him, eyes narrowing as he tried to gauge Ash's reaction.

"Let's not make a scene here, son," Harris said quietly, but his words carried an undeniable edge. "If you don't mind, we'd appreciate it if you'd come down to the station to help us understand what's go-ing on."

Ash forced himself to stay composed, trying to keep his breathing steady. The thought of the police walking into his house, seeing the rooms he'd so desperately tried to clean, made his skin crawl. But the fear of them discovering the truth clawed at him even more fiercely. He was in too deep now—he couldn't turn back. So, with a nod and a mask of indifference, he rose from his stool and followed them out of the bar.

In the car, he kept his gaze fixed on the road ahead, his heart pounding with each mile closer to the station. Ash tried to remember what he could—any detail that might help him survive the questioning he knew was coming. He reminded himself of the lie he'd tried to be-lieve, even if only for a moment: that he had no memory of the night before. It was the only shield he had left.

As they pulled into the station, Ash knew he was walking into a labyrinth of questions, suspicion, and answers he didn't know if he'd be able to fabricate. All he could do was pray that his tangled web would hold, even as it threatened to collapse around him with every step.

Ten

Ash sat in the frigid interrogation room, his hands restless and awkward, unsure where to put them. He'd always heard that looking nervous made people seem guilty, but trying not to look nervous somehow made it worse. His fingers tapped out a rhythm on the table, betraying his agitation, until he forced them to still, clasping them tightly in his lap.

Detective Harris leaned forward, his gaze unwavering and stern. "So, Ash. Where were you Saturday night?"

Ash cleared his throat, pushing down the knot of anxiety swelling inside him. "I was at the bar. I saw my parents earlier—they went out to dinner with friends. I went to the bar after they left."

He clung to the half-truth, knowing it would only hold if he kept his answers vague. Detective Harris seemed to read every twitch of Ash's face, every glance of his eyes, and Ash felt a sickening weight settling in his stomach. Harris's voice was calm but sharp, slicing through Ash's defenses.

Detective Schultz returned, setting a bottle of water in front of Ash with a soft thud, and offered a friendly nod before taking his seat across from him. But any sense of relief Ash might have felt disappeared when Harris continued with a string of pointed questions.

"Your sisters," Harris pressed, "when did you last see them?"

Ash hesitated, eyes darting to the one-way mirror on the wall. He swallowed hard. "Chelsea... I dropped her off for school practice Saturday morning. I didn't see Anna at all on Saturday. She was probably at a friend's or... something."

"Or something?" Harris's voice was flat, laced with disbelief. The seconds ticked by, the silence stretching, as the detective watched him with unblinking intensity. Ash could feel his story crumbling under that stare, his lies splintering, no matter how much he tried to stitch them together.

Hours bled into each other as they circled the same questions, each interrogation detail prying deeper into Ash's thinning resolve. Detective Schultz, the "good cop," would step in with an occasional kind word, offering Ash moments of reprieve before Harris resumed, his relentless grilling slicing through Ash's every line of defense. It was an unending cycle of exhaustion and tension, and Ash was running out of answers.

Just as his nerves threatened to snap entirely, Detective Harris's phone buzzed, a sharp interruption in the stillness. Harris glanced at it, his eyes widening in surprise. He stood up, signaling to Schultz, who quickly followed him out of the room. Ash watched them leave, his heart pounding as the door clicked shut behind them.

A chill ran down his spine as he heard snippets of voices from the hallway. He couldn't make out everything, but he caught two words that sent his world spinning.

"Chelsea's *alive*."

Eleven

A jolt of panic surged through Ash. He had no idea where Chelsea had been, or what she might know. The possibility of her turning up alive—someone who could remember, who could recount every horror of that night, and who could place him at the scene of the crime—made his pulse hammer.

After a few long minutes, the door opened, and Harris and Schultz walked back in, their expressions unreadable. Harris leaned forward, folding his hands together.

"Ash," he said, his voice cold and steady, "we've located your sister, Chelsea. She's been in contact with us, and she's safe. I think it's time for you to tell us everything."

Ash's vision swam as he stared into the hard lines of Harris's face. The room felt like it was closing in on him, the walls pressing down, his lies finally unraveling. He opened his mouth to speak, but words failed him. The horror of the truth—or, at least, the pieces he could remember—rose in his throat, almost choking him.

As Harris waited, eyes narrowing with a keen, relentless expectation, Ash knew there was no escape now.

Twelve

Chelsea opened her eyes to pitch darkness, her mind thick with confusion. As the musty scent seeped into her senses, a pang of realization dawned on her. Her wrists and ankles throbbed from the tightness of the tape that bound them, and her lips pressed painfully against the adhesive strip that muffled her mouth. She fought the rising tide of panic and focused on assessing her surroundings.

Where am I? she thought, her heart pounding against her rib-cage.

Shadows took shape around her as her eyes adjusted, and she recognized, with a chill of disbelief, that she was in the attic of her own house. The dim light filtering through a tiny, dust-coated window confirmed it. Memories from the night before surged back, jumbled and terrifying. She didn't know how she'd ended up there, bound and gagged, but something dark and monstrous had crept into her home, turning everything upside down.

Instead of dwelling on the fear and questions clawing at her mind, Chelsea forced herself to focus on freeing herself. She twisted her wrists back and forth, wincing as the tape dug into her skin. After several excruciating minutes, she finally worked her hands free. With trembling fingers, she peeled the tape from her mouth, gasping as fresh air filled her lungs.

She bit down on a scream and, with quiet resolve, freed her ankles. She glanced around the cramped attic, heart pounding in her throat, and spotted the closed trapdoor that led down into the house. She made her way to it, her fingers tracing its edges. She pushed, rattling it slightly, but it was locked tight.

"Mom? Dad? Anna?" she called out, her voice thick with desperation, but her words vanished into the silence.

Chelsea tried the small window, tugging at the frame until it cracked open slightly. She pressed her mouth against it and screamed, hoping against hope that someone outside might hear. But the neighborhood was still, the only response the faint stir of the night air.

Hours passed in that stale darkness, each minute stretching agonizingly longer than the last. She fought to keep herself calm, but every sound in the empty house seemed to crawl through the walls, taunting her. She drifted in and out of fitful sleep, jolting awake at every creak and groan.

Then, just as dawn broke, a muffled sound reached her ears—voices, faint but real, drifting from the floor below. Her heart raced. Someone was in the house.

Desperate, Chelsea pounded her fists against the floor, screaming with every ounce of strength she had left. She strained to hear, catching fragments of conversation.

"She's in the attic!"

A surge of relief washed over her as the trapdoor creaked open. A flashlight beam pierced the dim attic, and Chelsea's eyes adjusted just in time to see a woman with a kind face and a gentle smile. She wore a police uniform, her blonde hair pulled back into a low bun.

The officer stepped forward, her voice soft yet steady. "I'm Officer Kelly. It's okay, honey. I'm here to help you."

The kindness in her voice broke through Chelsea's last defenses, and she collapsed, sobbing, as Officer Kelly crossed the attic to wrap her in a warm embrace. Through her tears, Chelsea clung to her, feeling a flicker of safety at last.

As Officer Kelly led her down the attic steps, her soothing words filled the air, reassuring Chelsea that everything would be okay. But as Chelsea took in the stark silence of the empty house, a shiver ran down her spine. She couldn't shake the feeling that her nightmare was only just beginning.

Thirteen

Chelsea lay in the hospital bed, the white sheets a stark contrast to the dried blood on her head. She winced as a nurse checked the wound on her scalp, her wrists and ankles raw and marked where the tape had been. Physically, she was fine, but mentally, she felt like she was unraveling.

When the detectives arrived, they were far gentler than they'd been with Ash. She was just a young girl, caught in something horrific, and they could see the fragility behind her eyes. They waited a moment, letting her gather herself, and then asked if she was ready to talk. Chelsea asked to go home, desperate to leave the sterile hospital room, but they gently explained that her house was closed off, the investigation still ongoing.

After a deep breath, Chelsea began. "After volleyball practice, my sister picked me up, and we went to lunch at Maxwell's over on Corporate Drive. Afterward, we stopped at the Busy Bee Flea Market, just browsing around. When we got home, our parents weren't there. Mom had been at Stephanie's house, and Dad was probably out for a run."

Chelsea hesitated, her voice barely a whisper. "I was in my room reading when I heard them come home. I peeked out of my door, saw them going upstairs to shower and change—they had dinner plans with the Johnson's that night."

The detectives nodded, listening intently.

"After they got ready, they came into my room to say goodbye," she continued, her voice cracking slightly. "They said they'd see me later. I think Anna had gone out with friends, and Ash... well, I figured he was at his usual spot, Hunters bar."

The room was silent as Chelsea pieced together the evening. "I went back to reading, and at some point, I must have fallen asleep. I woke up to the sound of what I thought was gunshots. I was so scared, I ran to my door and locked it, then hid in the closet."

She swallowed, her hands trembling slightly. "I heard someone outside my room. They knocked first, then tried the handle, but it was locked. I thought they'd give up. But a few minutes later, I heard the sound of a key in the lock. I... I used to keep a spare key hidden under my dresser. Someone must have known about it, found it, and taken it without me realizing it was gone."

The detectives exchanged glances, leaning in closer.

"They opened the door," Chelsea said, her voice now thick with fear and pain. "I held my breath, trying not to make a sound, but they opened the closet. I screamed, and then... then they hit me. I felt the pain, and everything went dark. When I woke up, I was in the attic, tied up."

One of the detectives gently placed a hand on her shoulder. "You were incredibly brave, Chelsea," he said softly. "You did everything you could to stay safe."

As Chelsea finished her account, her mind replayed the terrifying memories, each one sharper than the last. She thought of her parents and Anna, wondering if they'd been safe or if she'd lost them forever. A deep sadness filled her eyes.

The detectives exchanged looks as they took in Chelsea's story. Chelsea's account raised new questions, but one thing was certain: someone wanted her family gone, and that same person had locked her away, trying to silence her. But why? And who would go to such lengths?

The room filled with a haunting quiet as Chelsea clutched the hospital sheets, her mind racing as she struggled to hold back tears. She couldn't help but wonder if she truly was safe now, or if the nightmare was far from over.

Fourteen

The detectives stood beside Chelsea's hospital bed, their voices low and cautious. "We're doing everything we can to locate your parents and sister, Chelsea. Anything else you remember, anything at all, could help us," one of them said gently. But Chelsea shook her head, her voice flat as she replied, "That's all I know."

Then she looked up at them, a hint of steel in her gaze. "Have you talked to my brother?" she asked.

The detectives exchanged a glance before one of them nodded. "He's being questioned," he replied.

Chelsea took a deep breath. "It's him. He did this. It's all his fault." Her words dropped heavily, leaving the detectives silent as they absorbed her accusation.

"What do you mean?" one detective asked, his tone probing yet soft.

"I know my brother," she said, her voice trembling with a mix of anger and sadness. "I know what he's capable of. He knows what happened to my parents, and he knows where they are. Whatever he's told you... don't believe him." Her words, chillingly certain, hung in the air, and the detectives nodded before quietly exiting her room, leaving her alone.

As the door closed behind them, Chelsea exhaled deeply, her exhaustion consuming her. She closed her eyes, finally surrendering to the sleep her body craved, letting the hospital's sterile silence engulf her.

When she awoke, sunlight streamed through the window. She reached for the remote and turned on the small TV in her room. A breaking news banner ran across the screen, and as the newscaster's voice filled the room, Chelsea sat up, watching in stunned silence.

Footage showed her brother, Ash, being led out of a police station, his hands cuffed behind him, surrounded by officers. The newscaster's voice was steady but grave. *"Twenty-year-old Ash Mitchell has been arrested in connection with the slaying of his family. Sources say he is the primary suspect, though authorities are still investigating."*

Chelsea's hand flew to her mouth, her eyes widening as she absorbed the reality of what she was seeing. But as the shock settled, her expression shifted, and an unmistakable smirk crept across her face.

Fifteen

Ash sat in the dimly lit room, hands shackled to the table. His court-appointed attorney had just laid out the grim reality: there was overwhelming evidence against him, and the only real option left was to plead insanity. The words hung in the air like a death sentence.

"But I didn't do it," Ash muttered, his voice thick with frustration. "I can't remember anything, but I know I wouldn't hurt them. I wouldn't hurt my family."

The attorney sighed, giving him a sympathetic but resigned look. "They have blood evidence from your parents' bedroom, from Anna's bedroom. Chelsea identified you as the suspect. They've even recovered a pistol from your home—the gun that matches the bullet casings found. They're testing it for fingerprints, but... Ash, the odds are stacked against you."

Ash swallowed hard, his hands balled into fists. Everything felt surreal, like he was trapped in someone else's nightmare. "I just... I need to talk to Chelsea. She's lying, she has to be lying," he whispered. His mind raced, trying to make sense of why his own sister would turn against him like this.

The attorney's eyes softened. "I'll make a request. They might allow a monitored call."

Hours later, he was led to a small, isolated room where a phone had been set up on the table. After a moment, a guard dialed the number and stepped out, leaving Ash alone. The phone rang several times before a soft voice finally answered.

"Hello?"

"Chelsea?" Ash said, his voice shaking. He gripped the receiver tightly, bracing himself. "Chelsea, it's me. Why did you do this? Why are you telling them it was me?"

There was a silence on the other end before Chelsea's voice broke through, cold and detached. "Because it was you, Ash. Who else would it be?"

"Chelsea, I don't remember anything," Ash pleaded, feeling the anger and despair rise in his throat. "I know I wouldn't hurt you... or Mom, or Dad. I don't know what happened that night, but I swear to you, I didn't do this."

A low chuckle came from Chelsea's end of the line, sending a chill down Ash's spine. "I don't know what's worse, Ash—the fact that you did it or the fact that you can't even remember it."

His breath caught, and he tightened his grip on the receiver. "Chelsea, why? Why are you lying?"

Her voice turned icy, dripping with resentment. "You think you're innocent, don't you? You think you've been the perfect son, the perfect brother. But you don't remember, Ash. You don't remember the anger you felt, the way you looked at me that night. You were out of control."

Ash felt his heart pounding. "No... no, that can't be true. You're making this up. Chelsea, please."

But Chelsea's only response was silence. Finally, she whispered, "Goodbye, Ash." The line clicked, and she was gone.

Ash stared at the phone, feeling hollow. He had hoped that Chelsea might reveal the truth, that somehow, she could help him remember what happened that night. But now, he was left only with a growing dread that she was right, that maybe he was capable of something unthinkable—and that the truth was even darker than he dared to imagine.

Sixteen

Ash sat on his bunk, staring at the cracked concrete wall in front of him. The noise of the prison was constant—the distant clank of metal doors, the murmur of inmates' conversations, the occasional shout. It had been years since he had been sentenced, years since that night of chaos and blood, and yet the weight of it never left him. In some ways, he had become accustomed to the life he now led. Prison had become his new normal. The routine, the isolation, the monotony—they had all settled into a strange, quiet rhythm.

But there was no escaping the memories. No matter how much time had passed, the flashes of that night still tormented him. The fragmented images—his parents' dismembered bodies, Anna's shallow grave, the sickening sound of dragging the bins to the shed—it was all a blur that he could never piece together fully. He hated it. Sometimes, in the dead of night, when sleep came too easily, the visions would resurface. He could feel the weight of his sister's lifeless body in his arms, the sickeningly warm blood on his hands. It would overwhelm him, forcing him to wake with a jolt, drenched in sweat, desperate to shake the memories away.

His life in prison had become a constant cycle of guilt and regret. There were days when he found himself asking if he could have done things differently. If he had only listened to his parents, held down a steady job, avoided the drugs and alcohol that had clouded his judgment, would things have turned out differently? Could he have avoided the horrible choice2s that led him here?

The memories came unbidden, the tension of growing up in the polished affluence of Old Westbury. His parents had worked tirelessly to keep up appearances, pushing him and his sisters relentlessly to succeed, to maintain the façade of a perfect family in a neighborhood where success wasn't just admired—it was expected. The house had been a pressure cooker of expectations: perfect grades, elite colleges, prestigious jobs. Every missed benchmark felt like a catastrophe.

The stress had been constant, the air at home thick with tension. Even as a kid, Ash had felt it—the undercurrent of desperation as his parents strove to belong, to prove they were worthy of their zip code. He'd watched it weigh down his sisters, too, and had eventually cracked under the pressure himself.

But that was all in the past now, wasn't it? He had to face the hard truth: there was no going back. No undoing what had been done.

Ash flinched as the sound of his name echoed through the hallway. A guard was standing at his cell door, an unreadable expression on his face. "You have a visitor," the guard said. "Who is it?"

Ash blinked, confused. Visitors were rare. His family was gone, and though some distant relatives had come once or twice, they never stuck around. Who could it possibly be? The guard shrugged, not offering any further details.

"Alright," Ash mumbled, standing up and shuffling toward the door.

He stepped into the visiting area, feeling a strange knot tighten in his stomach. As he approached the small, glass-walled cubicle, he caught sight of the visitor sitting at the table. His heart skipped a beat.

It was Chelsea.

Seventeen

Ash sat in the sterile, gray room, his eyes trained on the door as he waited. His heart hammered in his chest, a nervous rhythm he couldn't shake, even after all these years. He never thought he'd see Chelsea again—not like this. Not after everything that had happened.

The door swung open with a soft creak, and in walked his sister, Chelsea. Ash's breath hitched. She looked different, older. There was a hardness to her face, an edge that hadn't been there before. And then he saw it—the slight curve of her belly beneath her coat. His mind briefly stopped, confused.

"Ash," she said flatly as she took a seat across from him, her gaze unwavering. "Yes, I'm pregnant."

The words hung in the air between them, unspoken tension thickening the space. Ash didn't know how to react. Was he supposed to congratulate her? Apologize again for everything that had happened?

But Chelsea didn't give him the chance to say anything. She looked at him, her eyes cold, distant, as if she had already moved past him, past all of it.

"I'm not here to forgive you," she said bluntly. "I'm not here to tell you about my life, because you don't deserve that. I'm here because I want you to know that this will be the last time you'll see me. Ever."

Ash's heart sank, but he didn't know what to say. The words she spoke were final, leaving no room for anything else.

"Mom and Dad's money," she continued, her voice devoid of emotion. "The house—I decided to sell it. I'm moving to Colorado. I just thought you should know."

Ash stared at her, trying to process the information. She was leaving—leaving it all behind. Leaving him behind.

She paused, as if waiting for a reaction, but Ash remained silent. What could he say? Nothing could change what had already been done, and he knew it.

Chelsea's eyes softened for just a moment, but there was still that distance between them. "I know you'll never remember anything from that night," she added quietly, her voice almost too calm. "But that's not my problem. It's yours."

The words felt like a punch to the gut, but Ash just nodded.

"I'm happy for you, Chels," he said softly, his voice barely above a whisper.

Chelsea looked at him, her expression unreadable. Her eyes searched his face for something—maybe for sincerity, maybe for the old brother she used to know—but she didn't find it.

"Are you?" she asked, her tone laced with doubt. "Are you really happy for me?"

Ash swallowed hard, unsure of what to say. He wasn't sure if he was happy for her, or if he was just numb to it all. He hadn't even been able to remember what happened that night—what he had done.

But it didn't matter anymore, did it? She had made up her mind.

Chelsea stood up, her hand resting briefly on her stomach. For a moment, her gaze softened, but only for a fleeting second before she turned away.

"Goodbye, Ash," she said quietly, her voice breaking just a little. But when she looked back, there was no more hesitation, no more looking back.

As she walked out the door, Ash stayed seated, his mind reeling with everything she had said. This was the end. He had lost her for good. No amount of apologies, no amount of regret could change that.

He had lost her. And now, all he could do was sit in the silence of his cell, trapped in the unrelenting nightmare of his own making, knowing that nothing would ever be the same again.

Eighteen

Chelsea stood on the front porch of the house she had grown up in, staring at the familiar, aged brick façade. The memories of what had happened here—of the tragedy that had shattered her family—felt distant now, almost like a dream. This house, the place where she'd once felt the warmth of her parents' love, where she'd laughed and fought with her siblings, was now a tomb of the past. It was funny, in a way, that she would never have to look at it again.

She felt a soft pressure on her belly, and her eyes drifted down to where her husband's hand rested gently. She smiled at him, the man who had helped her heal in more ways than she could count, and whispered, "Let's go."

Without a second glance, they turned away from the house and headed toward their car. The air felt different today, as if it was filled with both the weight of everything she was leaving behind and the hope of everything that was to come.

They drove to the airport, the city fading behind them, the memories and ghosts of that old life becoming smaller with each mile. As the plane took off, Chelsea gazed out the window, her heart heavy yet somehow lighter than it had been in years. Colorado was waiting for them—a fresh start, a new chapter.

After the tragedy, Chelsea had been raised by her grandparents, who loved her as much as they possibly could. They gave her a sense of stability when everything else in her life had fallen apart. School was different now, too. She no longer felt the crushing weight of expectations from her parents. There were no more late-night discussions about perfect grades or the pressure to be the best at everything she did. For the first time in her life, she could breathe.

Her life was quieter now, but still, people couldn't help but ask questions. How was she coping with everything? How had she managed to put the pieces of her life back together after all that had happened?

Chelsea smiled at them, always brushing the questions aside, changing the subject to avoid the pain of digging into her past. People began to accept that she wasn't ready to talk, and they learned to leave it at that. But some still wondered. Something in the way Chelsea carried herself, something in her eyes, made them think there was more she wasn't saying. They just couldn't put their finger on it.

Among those who couldn't let go of the past was Stephanie, her mother's friend. Stephanie had always been curious, but after the murder of Chelsea's family, she became almost obsessed with the case. While she despised Ash for what he'd done, it was Chelsea who intrigued her the most. Stephanie sensed that Chelsea held more answers than she let on—secrets that she was keeping buried deep inside.

Unable to accept the conclusion of the case, Stephanie hired a private investigator to dig deeper. While the evidence overwhelmingly pointed to Ash as the murderer, Stephanie was not convinced. There had to be something more. Something she hadn't been told.

Then, word got out that Chelsea was moving to Colorado, and it raised a red flag for Stephanie. Everyone else saw it as Chelsea's way of escaping the painful past, but to Stephanie, it seemed like something else. Chelsea wasn't just leaving a house behind—she was leaving her grandparents, the only family she had left, and the cemetery where her parents and sister were buried.

Stephanie began to suspect that Chelsea's move was more than just a fresh start—it was a way to get away from something else. But what?

Chelsea's plane ascended into the sky, and she glanced one last time at the city below. As the world below grew smaller, she whispered softly to herself, "Goodbye." She was saying goodbye to the house, to the memories, to the past that had defined her for so long.

But as the miles stretched between her and her old life, she knew—her old life would follow her. Even in Colorado, she couldn't outrun it.

Nineteen

Chelsea was 32 now, and her life seemed far removed from the tragedy that had once defined her. She was married to Jonathan, and they had a 15-year-old daughter, Sofia, who was the spitting image of Chelsea in some ways but, in other ways, a reflection of Jonathan. Sofia had her mother's blonde hair, but her father's strong jaw and demeanor. However, there was one feature that reminded Chelsea of something she couldn't escape—the hazel eyes, just like Ash's. Every time she looked into Sofia's eyes, something in her twisted. She hated the reminder of Ash, the brother she had left behind, the murderer she wished she could forget. But it was there, in Sofia's gaze.

Sofia came downstairs to the dinner table, her chatter filling the room as she placed herself at her seat. "Mom, this chicken is delicious!" she exclaimed, her voice bubbling with energy. Chelsea smiled and nodded absently, distracted by her own thoughts, her fingers gripping the edge of her plate a little too tightly.

"Glad you like it," Chelsea said, trying to keep her focus on the meal.

Sofia continued talking about her day at school, about her friends, about the drama at lunch. Jonathan, sitting across from her, merely glanced up every so often, shaking his head like he was listening even though his eyes were focused on his plate. He wasn't much of a talker, and Chelsea had long since learned to fill in the silence. She'd ask Sofia questions, trying to engage her in conversation, but her mind kept wandering back to the fact that her life—everything she'd built—was eerily similar to what she'd once vowed she would never create.

As Chelsea asked Sofia if she'd finished her homework, Sofia gave her a quick nod, then paused. "Oh, wait, Mom," she said. "We have a family tree project. It's due next week."

Chelsea's heart skipped a beat. Family tree. It felt like a thorn had been lodged right into her chest. She looked up at Sofia, her face a mask of calm, but inside she was already spiraling.

"A family tree project?" Chelsea asked, her voice slightly unsteady.

Sofia nodded eagerly, a bit of excitement in her voice. "Yeah, everyone in my class is talking about it. They're showing off their family trees, like, with their grandparents, cousins, aunts, and uncles. It's so cool! I don't really know much about our family, though. Is that weird?"

Chelsea's stomach clenched. She had avoided this conversation for years. Sofia's questions, innocent and full of curiosity, were becoming more frequent, and this project, with its demands for details, was forcing her hand. Chelsea's mind raced as she tried to steer the conversation elsewhere.

"No, it's not weird," Chelsea said, trying to keep her voice steady. "It's just... you know, our family is small. We've just got your father and me."

Jonathan raised an eyebrow at the mention of family, his usual indifference giving way to the slightest flicker of interest. But it quickly faded as he turned his attention back to his plate, pushing the food around without much enthusiasm.

Sofia continued, oblivious to the tension building in her mother. "But Mom, where are my grandparents? Don't we have any aunts and uncles?"

Chelsea's breath caught in her throat. For a moment, the world felt suffocating, like the walls were closing in on her. How could she explain it to Sofia? How could she answer these questions when she had spent so many years avoiding them herself?

Sofia's face shifted from enthusiasm to confusion, her innocent curiosity meeting the silent wall of her mother's resistance. "What happened to them, Mom?"

Chelsea's heart pounded in her chest, and for the first time in a long while, she felt a deep sense of regret. She had made a life for Sofia—a life that was supposed to be free of the dark legacy she had carried with her—but now, here it was, creeping back into their world, demanding answers.

Chelsea tried to smile, though it felt like a mask she couldn't quite wear. "It's... it's complicated, honey. I just... don't think you need to worry about it. Your family is right here, and that's all that matters. We're a team, right?"

Sofia seemed to sense her mother's discomfort, but she didn't press further. She looked down at her plate, pushing the food around absently. But something had shifted in her—there was a quiet sadness in her eyes, a sense that the pieces of her family didn't quite fit together, and she didn't know why.

Chelsea's thoughts raced. She couldn't let Sofia dig too deeply. She couldn't let her know everything.

As the meal continued, Chelsea tried to focus on the present, but the weight of her past pressed down on her with every passing second. How much longer could she keep up the charade? How much longer could she shield Sofia from the truth?

Sofia might not understand it now, but one day, those questions would come again. And when they did, Chelsea knew she wouldn't be able to hide behind the walls she'd built forever.

Twenty

The next day at school, Sofia sat at her desk, her mind swirling with thoughts of the family tree project. It was the topic of the day, and as the other kids eagerly shared their family stories, Sofia felt a tight knot form in her stomach. Her classmates couldn't wait to present their family histories—Molly proudly talked about her grandparents, aunts, uncles, and cousins. Joey shared an exciting tale about his grandfather, a former fireman who had risked his life to save a family from a burning building. Amber talked about her cousin, who was her best friend. But when it was Sofia's turn, she froze. She had nothing to share beyond her parents.

"Yup, just us," she said softly, not meeting anyone's gaze.

Her teacher nodded politely, accepting Sofia's family tree as it was, but the other kids weren't as understanding. They leaned forward, their curiosity piqued.

"Wait, so you don't have any grandparents?" one of the kids asked, his tone a little too loud.

"What about an aunt or uncle? Or cousins? Second cousins?" another added, their voice laced with disbelief.

The teacher, sensing Sofia's discomfort, quickly stepped in. "Alright, everyone, let's calm down. Every family is different, and Sofia's is just as unique as any other." She gave Sofia a reassuring smile. "It's okay, Sofia. Thank you for sharing."

Sofia nodded, a faint blush creeping onto her cheeks as the other students fell silent. She hoped the questioning would stop, but she felt their eyes on her as she sank lower into her chair. She just wanted to get through the day and avoid any more questions.

When school finally ended, Sofia couldn't shake the feeling that something was off. She had no idea about her family's history outside her immediate parents. It felt like a part of her had been missing her whole life, and now, with the family tree project looming over her, she couldn't ignore it anymore. She needed answers.

As soon as she got home, she went straight to her room, determined to find out whatever she could. She didn't expect her mom to tell her the truth anytime soon, so she took matters into her own hands. She opened her laptop and typed "Mitchell family Colorado" into the search bar. Nothing. No leads. No information. Nothing that could answer her questions.

But then, on a whim, she typed in her mom's full name: *Chelsea Marie Mitchell.* The moment she hit enter, a slew of articles appeared on the screen—most of them were old news stories. Sofia's heart began to race. She clicked on the first article, which was a brief mention of a tragic event—a gruesome murder that had occurred years ago. The more she read, the more her stomach twisted in knots. The article mentioned her mother, Chelsea, and a horrific incident involving Chelsea's family. It spoke of the deaths of her parents and her sister. But no details about Sofia. Nothing that explained the mystery of her family.

Suddenly, Sofia heard the front door open. Her breath caught in her throat as she quickly closed the laptop and shoved it under her bed. Her mother's voice echoed from downstairs, calling her name.

"Sofia? Are you home?"

Sofia quickly stood up and went downstairs, trying to act normal. Chelsea was standing by the door, taking off her coat, her eyes searching Sofia's face as if she could sense something was wrong.

"How was school?" Chelsea asked, her voice light but with an edge that Sofia couldn't ignore.

Sofia shrugged nonchalantly, not wanting to give anything away. "It was fine."

Chelsea raised an eyebrow. "How did the family tree project go?"

Sofia hesitated for a moment. She thought about the questions from her classmates, the articles she had just discovered, but she kept quiet. "It went well," she said, though it felt like a lie hanging on her lips.

Chelsea nodded, seemingly satisfied. But then Sofia remembered the message she had overheard before, the phone call that had come in while her mother was still at work.

"Oh, someone named Stephanie called for you," Sofia said casually, trying to sound as nonchalant as possible. "She wanted to speak with you."

The moment the name left her lips, Chelsea's face fell. The color drained from her cheeks, and for a brief second, her eyes flickered with something—something deep and unsettling.

"What... what did she want?" Chelsea asked, her voice low, a tension creeping into it that Sofia had never heard before.

Sofia's heart raced as she watched her mother's reaction. There was something about the way Chelsea had asked that made Sofia's stomach twist. What could Stephanie possibly want? And why had her mom's reaction been so... alarmed?

"I don't know," Sofia said, trying to keep her voice steady. "She just wanted to talk to you. But you weren't home."

Chelsea nodded slowly, her eyes distant now. "Thank you for letting me know," she said quietly, her voice betraying a hint of something Sofia couldn't place. "I'll call her back."

As Chelsea walked past her toward the kitchen, Sofia stood still, her mind spinning. The name *Stephanie* echoed in her thoughts, but it was the way her mother had reacted—so unexpectedly—that made Sofia's chest tighten. There was something she wasn't telling her, something important.

Sofia made a silent vow to herself then. She was going to find out who *Stephanie* was, and she was going to get the answers to the questions that had been haunting her for so long. She might not have the whole family tree, but she knew one thing for sure—there were secrets buried deep, and she was going to uncover them.

Twenty One

Later that evening, after dinner, when the house had quieted down and everyone had settled into their own activities, Chelsea couldn't shake the feeling of unease that had been creeping up on her all day. She had a strange, inexplicable sense that things were unraveling, that the past she had worked so hard to bury was coming back to the surface.

Sitting alone in the dimly lit living room, Chelsea glanced at the phone on the table. Her fingers itched to pick it up, and after a brief hesitation, she did. She scrolled through the contacts, her heart pounding as she found Stephanie's number. The memories of their past interactions, of the relentless questioning, the accusations, and the painful silence that had followed, flooded back.

She hesitated, then dialed the number.

The phone rang several times before it clicked, and Chelsea held her breath as the line connected.

"Hello?" Stephanie's voice came through, sharp and clear, as if she'd been waiting for this call.

Chelsea's heart skipped a beat. She knew she wasn't ready for this conversation, but she couldn't stop herself. "Hi," Chelsea said, trying to keep her voice steady. "I saw that you called."

"Oh, yes," Stephanie replied, her tone flat but inquisitive. "How did you get my number?" Chelsea said.

Stephanie paused, unsure how to answer. She didn't want to say it had been a simple matter of digging through old files, tracking down a few leads. Instead, she forced out an almost casual response. "It wasn't easy, but don't worry about that."

"Alright then," Chelsea said, as if brushing off Stephanie's words. "I called you because... do you remember the night your parents and sister tragically passed?"

Chelsea's stomach churned at the mention of that night. She had worked so hard to push the memories away, to bury them deep where they couldn't hurt her. But hearing it again, from Stephanie's mouth, brought it all rushing back.

"I try not to think about it every day," Chelsea said, her voice growing tight.

Stephanie's next words were like a cold slap. "Well, I just have one question: How come your brother killed your entire family except you? Have you ever thought about that? How weird it was that he kept you alive and not the rest of your family?"

Chelsea's heart stopped. She felt her chest tighten, panic bubbling up in her throat. She had always known that the questions surrounding that night were still out there, that people still had suspicions, but hearing them spoken aloud, coming from Stephanie—someone who had always seemed to sense more than she should—was too much.

Chelsea swallowed hard, her mind racing. "Not really," she said, trying to sound indifferent. "Stephanie, is this really why you're calling right now? I haven't spoken to you in years. I'd really appreciate it if you didn't just... call me like this. If you have any questions about the murder of my family, I think you should ask those questions elsewhere, because like I said... I don't have any answers for you."

There was a brief silence on the other end of the line, and Chelsea could almost feel Stephanie's smirk through the phone.

"Alright, Chelsea," Stephanie said, her voice laced with an unsettling calmness. "But you should know... I'm not done asking questions. And I won't stop until I get the answers."

Chelsea felt a chill run down her spine, a creeping sense of dread that made her blood run cold. She didn't know what Stephanie meant by that, but the implication was clear—Stephanie wasn't going to let this go. And neither would anyone else who had questions about that night. Chelsea had always known the truth would eventually come out, but now, the weight of it all felt like it was crashing down on her, threatening to expose everything she had carefully hidden for years.

She ended the call abruptly, her hands shaking as she hung up the phone. The room felt colder now, the silence louder.

As Chelsea sat in the darkness, a knot of anxiety tightened in her stomach. She couldn't escape the feeling that everything she had built, the life she had created in Colorado, the walls she had erected around her family, were beginning to crack. It wasn't just Stephanie anymore—her daughter Sofia was starting to ask questions, too.

Sofia had started digging, pulling at the threads of a past Chelsea had tried so hard to erase. Her daughter's curiosity was growing, and Chelsea could see the same fire in Sofia's eyes that had once burned in her own when she had been younger, searching for answers. It was only a matter of time before Sofia would start asking the same dangerous questions Stephanie had asked.

Chelsea tried to steady her breath, but it was impossible. The walls she had so carefully constructed were crumbling, and there was nothing she could do to stop it. The truth, no matter how deeply buried, had a way of resurfacing—and this time, it wasn't just haunting her.

It was coming for Sofia too.

Twenty Two

Sofia sat cross-legged on her bed, her laptop glowing softly in the dim room as she scrolled through article after article, reading each word with a mix of horror and fascination. She couldn't believe what she was finding—the story was unimaginable, something out of a nightmare. Yet every line, every picture, and every headline reminded her that it wasn't a story. This was her family. This was her legacy.

Each page revealed more gruesome details: how her uncle Ash had murdered her grandparents and her aunt Anna in cold blood, how he had dismembered their bodies, burying pieces of them in the backyard. How he had dug a shallow grave for her aunt and hidden the evidence, all while her mother, Chelsea, had been locked up in the attic, helpless and alone.

Sofia's hand trembled as she clicked to the next page, a photo of the old house staring back at her. She'd seen pictures of the place before, but now it looked different—its walls and windows hiding secrets that had scarred her mother's life and, in turn, her own.

A flood of emotions crashed over her: confusion, anger, disbelief, sadness. It was clear now why her mother had never spoken about her family. The silence, the coldness around the topic—it all made sense. But what Sofia couldn't understand was how her mom had thought she'd never find out. She felt a growing resentment as she realized how little her mother trusted her with the truth.

And yet, there was a strange pull, a yearning to understand, to know more, to confront this hidden history face-to-face. Her uncle Ashe was still alive, locked up for life, but maybe he held the missing pieces. The horror of it all didn't scare her as much as she thought it would. Instead, she felt a new determination rising within her. Maybe if she could talk to him, she'd finally understand.

But she knew that if her mother found out, it would destroy the fragile trust between them. Sofia stared at the articles on her screen, chewing her lip as she thought it over. She'd have to be careful, quiet. She couldn't let her mom know.

Sofia's mind spun with the possibilities as she closed her laptop, but the words she'd read lingered, seared into her memory. That night, as she lay awake in the darkness, Sofia felt different—older, hardened. Her innocence was gone, replaced with a need to know.

No matter the cost, she was going to find out the *truth*.

Twenty Three

Sofia gripped the phone tightly, her palms clammy with nerves. She couldn't believe she was actually doing this—ditching volleyball practice, sneaking off to the library, and now trying to reach out to the man her mother had spent her life trying to forget.

Her stomach twisted as she dialed the number she'd found online for Holloway Correctional Facility. The call rang once before a curt, professional voice answered.

"Holloway Correctional Facility. This is Officer Ramirez. How can I assist you?"

Sofia froze, clutching the phone harder. "Uh... hi. I'm... I'm trying to get in touch with an inmate. His name is Ash Mitchell."

There was a brief pause, the sound of typing on a keyboard crackling faintly through the line. "And you are?"

"I'm..." She hesitated. What was she supposed to say? The niece he didn't know existed? "I'm his niece. Sofia."

Another pause, longer this time. She could practically hear Ramirez judging her through the phone. "He's not going to be able to call you directly unless you're on his approved contact list. Are you?"

"No, but—"

"Then you'll need to leave a message," Ramirez interrupted briskly. "We can notify him that you called, and he can decide if he wants to add you to his list. Otherwise, you won't be able to speak with him."

"No!" The word came out louder than she intended. She forced herself to take a steadying breath. "Please. I just... I just need to talk to him. Can you connect me? Just for a minute?"

The officer sighed, clearly irritated. "Hold on."

The line went quiet except for the faint hum of static. Sofia bit her lip, her heart hammering in her chest. What was she even going to say to him if this worked?

After what felt like an eternity, Ramirez's voice returned, now sharper. "You're lucky. He's agreed to talk. I'm putting you through, but keep it short."

There was a click, followed by a burst of static, and then a rough, unfamiliar voice filled her ear. "Yeah? Who's this?"

Sofia's throat went dry. This was it. She cleared her throat, her voice trembling as she finally managed to speak. "Um... hi. Is... is this Ash Mitchell?"

There was a pause, and then a low, almost bitter chuckle. "Depends on who's asking. Who are you?"

Sofia hesitated, but there was no turning back now. "I'm Sofia," she said finally, her voice barely a whisper. "Your niece."

The silence on the other end was thick. Ash seemed to be processing her words. She wondered if he even knew she existed. "Chelsea's daughter?" he asked slowly, his voice a strange mix of surprise and something else—regret, maybe.

"Yes." She took a shaky breath. "I... I wanted to talk to you. About what happened."

A heavy sigh escaped him, full of years and weight. "I don't know what to tell you, kid. I wish I could remember that night. Maybe it'd give me a chance to help you understand. But the truth is, I don't remember a damn thing," he said, his voice almost weary. "I was out of control, drinking and using whatever I could get my hands on. All that's left is regret."

Sofia's curiosity battled with a strange sadness. "So... you don't remember anything?"

"Not enough to put it together, not in a way that makes sense. If I could take it all back, I would," Ash said. "Prison's changed me. I know that sounds like some cliche, but it's true. I've had a lot of time to think, and I'd give anything to make things right. But it's too late for that now."

Sofia swallowed, taking in his words. "I just... I feel like there are pieces missing. Something my mom won't tell me."

Ash sighed. "Your mom... she's had her own way of dealing with all this, just like I have. But if you're looking for answers, there's someone you might want to talk to. Her name's Stephanie Jacobs, she used to be close to our family. She hated me for what happened, but over the years, she's come around to looking for the truth. She visits me sometimes, trying to piece together what happened."

Sofia's mind raced, and she scribbled down the name. "Stephanie Jacobs... Wait," she paused, her heart skipping a beat. "I remember that name. She called for my mom the other day."

"Yeah, that's her," Ash said, a hint of warmth breaking through the roughness in his voice. "She's been relentless, trying to get justice for the family. If anyone's going to help you figure this out, it's her."

Sofia nodded, the weight of her uncle's words settling over her. She didn't fully understand yet, but she had a feeling that whatever came next would change things.

Twenty Four

Sofia checked the clock—1:45. Her mom would be here any minute, and she was still blocks away from the school. She grabbed her things and darted out of the library, running so fast her backpack bounced against her shoulders. By the time she reached the school, her face was flushed, and her hair clung to her forehead. Just as she hoped, the exhaustion from sprinting made her look like she'd just finished volleyball practice.

Chelsea's car pulled up right on time, and Sofia slipped inside, hoping her breathless state would keep her mom from asking too many questions.

"You okay, honey?" Chelsea asked, noticing Sofia's hurried movements.

"Yeah, I'm just really hungry," Sofia replied quickly, eager to avoid any further probing.

Chelsea smiled, amused. "Tough practice, huh?"

"Yes," Sofia said, nodding, "can we get cheeseburgers?"

"Of course," Chelsea laughed, steering the car toward their favorite drive-thru. Sofia sank back in her seat, feeling her stomach twist—not from hunger, but from the flood of secrets she was carrying. In the past hour, she'd called her uncle, learned her family's darkest history, and found a connection to a mysterious woman who knew more than she'd ever imagined.

As the smell of hot fries filled the car, Sofia's actual hunger returned, and she popped a few into her mouth on the drive home, hoping they would settle her nerves. They got home, and Chelsea set their food out at the table. Sofia tried to relax, to act like she hadn't spent the past few days unraveling a lifetime of secrets.

"So, how was volleyball?" Chelsea asked, taking a bite of her burger.

Sofia forced a smile and shrugged. "It was fine," she said, her voice softer than usual. Normally, she'd dive into every little detail of her day, but today she felt like her words were heavy, fragile. She couldn't risk letting anything slip, not now.

Chelsea raised an eyebrow, noticing Sofia's uncharacteristic quiet. "Everything okay?" she asked gently.

"Yeah, I'm just tired," Sofia mumbled, picking at her fries. Inside, her thoughts swirled—part of her wanted to blurt everything out, to tell her mom that she knew, that she'd seen the articles, that she'd talked to her uncle. But she couldn't—not yet. There were still pieces missing, and until she had the full picture, she didn't want to reveal what she'd uncovered.

She looked at her mom, feeling a pang of guilt for hiding so much. But her curiosity wasn't finished; she wasn't ready to let this go.

Twenty Five

That night, Sofia lay in bed, her mind racing too fast for sleep. She felt as though a hundred unanswered questions swirled around her, growing louder the more she tried to ignore them. She needed a plan—a way to finally get some answers.

She thought about her parents, always home, always hovering, making it nearly impossible for her to search their room undisturbed. If only she could find a way to be alone in the house, even for just an hour or two. Maybe if she pretended to be sick this week, her mom would let her stay home. But Chelsea was strict about attendance, hardly letting her miss school for anything. Sofia sighed, feeling a pang of frustration.

With sleep nowhere in sight, Sofia grabbed her laptop and opened it quietly, searching for "Stephanie Jacobs." She quickly found an image: a glamorous woman with platinum-blonde hair, piercing blue eyes, and a face that looked both youthful and unnaturally smooth. The article revealed that Stephanie lived in Old Westbury, New York, in a sprawling mansion. Married to a wealthy accountant, she appeared to have a life of luxury, volunteering at the local garden center and attending charity events, all with an air of ease as if she'd never worked a day in her life.

"Stephanie," Sofia murmured, staring at the picture. *What do you know?*

Scrolling further, she found an email address. Her heart pounded as she debated whether to reach out. After a moment's hesitation, she opened a new message and began typing. She kept it short, carefully choosing her words:

Hi Stephanie,

My name is Sofia Mitchell. I'm Ash Mitchell's niece. I'm reaching out because I need help understanding some things about my family, and I think you might know more than I do. My mom doesn't know I'm contacting you, so please keep this between us.

Thank you,
Sofia

She took a deep breath, hit send, and stared at the screen, her mind reeling with the gravity of what she'd just done. Only eight minutes later, her laptop pinged with a new email. Her heart raced as she opened it, seeing a quick response from Stephanie.

Dear Sofia,

I've been waiting a long time for someone to reach out to me about this. There's much to discuss, but we need to be careful. Let's start slowly. What do you want to know?

Steph

Sofia's pulse quickened as she read the words, her hands trembling slightly. She was on the edge of finally learning the truth, of pulling together the pieces of her family's past. Taking a deep breath, she began typing her response, feeling both excitement and fear for whatever lay ahead.

Twenty Six

Sofia sat in the soft glow of her laptop, re-reading Stephanie's response over and over. Finally, she took a deep breath, fingers hovering over the keys as she carefully thought out her questions.

Her curiosity and frustration mingled, and she began typing, letting her questions flow out all at once.

Hi Stephanie,

Thanks for replying so quickly. I have so many questions, and I don't know where to start, but here goes:

First, how well did you know my family? What were my grandparents and Aunt Anna like? I never got to know them, and my mom never talks about them. She just says that it's painful, and that's why she doesn't share anything about them. I don't understand how she can keep everything so hidden from me, like I'd never want to know my own family.

Also, my uncle Ash…is he really a murderer? He told me on the phone that he doesn't remember anything from that night, and he regrets a lot of things. Is that true? Was he really so dangerous that he could hurt his own family, or is there something more that no one knows? I want to believe there's more to him than what I read online, but I don't know what to believe.

Uncle Ash mentioned that you're really curious about the case too, even though it was settled years ago. Why are you so eager to know more? What do you think happened? Why are you digging for information after all these years? Did you suspect something else?

And, if you don't mind me asking, how old were my aunt and uncle when this happened? I don't know any details about them, not even their ages or what their lives were like. I want to understand what really happened and who they were beyond what the news stories say.

I know this is a lot, but any answers you could give me would mean so much. Thank you for being willing to talk about it.

Sofia

Sofia hit send and slumped back, exhausted but determined. Now, all she could do was wait for Stephanie's next response and hope it would finally shed some light on the family secrets she was so desperate to uncover.

Twenty Seven

Sofia's laptop pinged with a new email. She felt a mix of excitement and nerves as she opened it, eager to read Stephanie's response.

Hi Sofia,

I'm glad you reached out to me. I know this must feel overwhelming, and I'll try to answer your questions as best as I can.

Your grandparents, June and Thomas Mitchell, were very respected and well-liked in our community. They were caring and warm people, and their lives were centered around their family. Your Aunt Anna was close with them, and they supported her in everything. She was 18 when...when everything happened. She had a bright future and was about to start college. Everyone who knew her adored her; she was funny, kind, and full of life.

Your Uncle Ash and your mother, Chelsea, were much younger back then, with Chelsea being the youngest sibling. Ash was 20, and Chelsea was only 16. She was so close to her family, and everyone in town felt so deeply for her when she was the only one left. I've seen her grow up carrying this weight, but maybe you can be the one to help her heal from the pain she's held onto.

As for Ash... it's complicated, Sofia. Yes, he was convicted, but he was young and, from what I understand, was going through a hard time with addiction. He's always claimed he can't remember that night and says that the drinking and drugs clouded his memory. Whether he's telling the truth, I don't know, but he's expressed regret over his actions and the choices that led him there. After so many years, it's hard to tell where the truth begins and ends.

Now, about why I still search for answers... Your mother's family was very dear to me, especially your grandparents. June was one of my closest friends, and I miss her every day. Maybe it's my own way of trying to make sense of what happened and bring justice to them, or maybe I just can't accept the loss. But there's a part of me that wonders if we'll ever fully understand what happened that night. It's not that I'm certain Ash was innocent, but sometimes things don't add up, and I'm not one to let go until I feel at peace with it.

Sofia, you're so young, and there are things I don't want to burden you with. I hope you understand that I have to keep certain details private. I'll share what I can, and if I come across anything that could help you make sense of this, I promise I'll tell you.

I wish you didn't have to go through all this, but maybe in time, you'll find the answers you're looking for. For now, try to be patient. And if you ever need to talk, I'm here.

Steph

Sofia finished reading, a mixture of satisfaction and frustration bubbling inside her. She understood Stephanie's hesitation and was grateful for the answers she did get. But it wasn't enough. There were still too many gaps.

She closed her laptop, determination building within her. If Stephanie wouldn't tell her everything, maybe she could find the missing pieces herself. She had to. And that meant searching her mom's room, whether her mom would approve or not.

Twenty Eight

Sunday night had settled in, casting a stillness over the house that made Sofia's nerves buzz with anticipation. She sat across from Chelsea in the dimly lit living room, feigning a tired, weary look as she clutched her stomach and winced slightly.

"I'm not feeling great, Mom," she murmured, hoping her voice sounded convincing enough.

Chelsea reached over, pressing her hand to Sofia's forehead. "You don't feel warm. Are you sure you're sick? Maybe it's just nerves about school tomorrow."

Sofia shrugged, hiding her true intentions behind a look of discomfort. "I don't know. I think I might need a day to rest."

Chelsea sighed, concern etched in her face, but her tone remained firm. "I can't stay home with you tomorrow, Sofia. I have an important meeting, and your father's working overtime at the hospital. Besides, you know how I feel about you staying home alone."

"But Mom," Sofia pressed, "I'll be fine. I'm not a little kid anymore."

"Sofia, we've talked about this. I don't feel comfortable with you staying home alone. And I'm not convinced you're actually sick," Chelsea said, her gaze narrowing. "I don't know why you're suddenly trying to get out of going to school. You've been acting...different lately. I've noticed it."

"Different?" Sofia echoed, trying to keep her voice steady.

"Yes, different." Chelsea's face softened but was edged with disappointment. "You've been distant with me, Sofia. You used to tell me everything, and now it feels like you're hiding things. Your grades have slipped—you're coming home with B's instead of A's. And your volleyball coach mentioned you missed practice on Saturday? I drove you there. So, where were you?"

Sofia's heart raced, but she kept her expression calm, hoping her mom wouldn't press too hard. She hadn't thought Chelsea knew about the missed practice.

"I just...wasn't feeling it," she said quietly, averting her eyes. "But, Mom...don't you think you're hiding things, too?"

Chelsea froze, her face suddenly unreadable. An uneasy silence hung between them, thick with unspoken words.

Twenty Nine

The next morning, Sofia stayed curled under her blankets, ignoring the usual morning rush as Chelsea called her down for breakfast, her voice growing more impatient with each call. Sofia's mind was still spinning from last night's conversation—her accusation about Chelsea hiding secrets had left a thick tension between them.

Finally, Chelsea's footsteps approached. Sofia squeezed her eyes shut, playing up the image of a sick, stubborn teenager.

"Sofia." Chelsea's voice was low and resigned. "Fine, you can stay home today. But promise me, from now on, no more slipping grades. No more missed volleyball practices. No more...secrets."

Sofia forced herself to sit up, her expression solemn. "I promise," she murmured, her heart pounding with the lie. Chelsea leaned down, giving her a gentle kiss on the forehead.

"I love you," Chelsea whispered before leaving the room, her voice wavering. Moments later, Sofia heard the front door open and close, followed by the hum of the SUV's engine in the driveway. She watched from her bedroom window as her mom glanced back toward the house. Sofia quickly ducked out of sight, her heart pounding as she waited for Chelsea to drive away.

When the coast was clear, Sofia wasted no time. She slipped out of bed, her steps silent as she crossed the hallway and stopped in front of her parents' locked bedroom door. Chelsea and her husband always kept it secured, but Sofia knew where the spare key was hidden—tucked beneath a loose floorboard in the hallway. She pried up the board and retrieved the small key, feeling a strange thrill as it fit perfectly into the lock.

The door opened, and a wave of her mom's familiar scent—lilacs and vanilla—washed over her. The room was immaculate, every item precisely in its place. Sofia's gaze darted around as she searched, lifting the bed skirt, pulling open closet doors, digging through drawers in the bathroom. But everything was spotless and meticulously organized, with no sign of the hidden past she was looking for.

After nearly an hour of searching, she sighed, feeling her hopes deflate. She sank down onto the plush carpet, defeated—until a subtle, almost invisible line caught her eye near the wall behind her mom's bedside table.

A small panel, blending into the wall, just barely visible. She shifted the end table aside and tapped on the tiny door, hearing a hollow echo. Her heart hammered as she wedged her fingers into the groove of the hidden panel and pulled it open.

Inside was a plain, unmarked box, slightly dusty, as if it hadn't been touched in years. She lifted it out carefully, staring at it in her hands. Whatever was inside, she knew, was a key to everything her mother had worked so hard to hide.

Thirty

Sofia's hands trembled as she slowly lifted the lid of the box. Inside, she found a stack of crumpled, yellowed newspaper clippings. Her heart raced as she shuffled through them, scanning headlines that were far too familiar—headlines detailing the tragic night of her family's murder, followed by more articles about the trial, with haunting images of her uncle Ash in handcuffs. The words blurred together as she read about the gruesome details of the crime, the defense team's arguments, the prosecutors' statements. It all felt like a dream, too surreal for Sofia to truly grasp.

But beneath the clippings, something heavier lay hidden—a thick, worn journal. Sofia's pulse quickened as she opened it, her eyes scanning the first page.

It was her mother's handwriting.

Sofia sat on the floor of the bedroom, the room feeling smaller and smaller as she flipped through the journal, her fingers trembling. Each entry revealed more of her mother's inner turmoil, building up to the fateful night that changed everything. The words grew darker, more bitter with each passing entry.

Then Sofia reached the entry dated April 27, 1998—the night her family was murdered.

Saturday, April 27, 1998

Dear diary,

I'm fed up with my parents. All they ask of me is to be perfect all the time. My brother is a lousy piece of crap, never home and always drunk, drinking away his lowlife self. My older sister thinks she's better than everyone, including me. Yeah, she takes me here and there, but deep down I hate her guts. My parents are the worst, though—constantly demanding perfection. All the time is not fun. I know I've said this in my journal entries, and I'll say it again. I hope they drop dead. Or maybe I could take matters into my own hands. Who would believe an innocent 16-year-old like myself would do harm to my family? No one. And I want to make sure of that. Once my brother goes out and gets blackout drunk at the same stupid bar he always goes to, I'll put his sweatshirt on, go and shoot my parents and my sister and make it look like my brother did it. Just hoping that it works.

Sofia's breath caught in her throat. She couldn't believe what she was reading. Her mind raced as she tried to process the words on the page. Her mother had planned this. She had been the one behind the murder.

But Sofia couldn't stop reading.

April 28th, 1998

It's done! My idiot brother came home and went straight to sleep. Little does he know that our parents are dead in their bed, and Anna is also dead in her bed. I took the gun, shot them, hit myself in the head with it real hard so that I bled, climbed up into the attic, and tied myself up. My brother is sound asleep right now. He got up for a second, didn't check on the family, of course, so he still doesn't have a clue what happened. But he'll find out sooner or later. I'll just put everything on him because he's a useless piece of crap anyway.

Sofia's stomach churned. Her mother's confession was written in cold, calculated detail. She couldn't believe what she was reading. But the truth was right in front of her, undeniable. Her mother had killed her own family, including her sister, Anna, and set up Ash to take the fall.

Sofia could hardly breathe as the weight of the journal settled in her lap. Her heart hammered against her chest. She wasn't sure what to do. Should she call the police? Would they believe her? How could she betray her own mother?

As she sat there, paralyzed by the confession in her hands, her phone rang, breaking the silence. Sofia jumped, startled by the noise, her pulse quickening. She glanced at the screen—her mother's name flashed across the display.

Sofia hesitated, the phone vibrating in her hand. She didn't know what to do. Should she answer? What would she even say?

But she knew she couldn't hide from the truth any longer.

Thirty One

Sofia stared at the phone in her hand as it rang a few more times. Her mind was racing. She didn't know what to do. Should she answer it? Should she lie? Could she keep her cool long enough to pretend everything was fine? What if her mom could somehow sense her fear? What if she had already noticed something was wrong?

As the phone rang a final time, Sofia knew she had no choice. She had to answer. She couldn't risk her mom becoming suspicious. Not now. Not when everything she thought she knew was crumbling around her.

"Hey, Mom," Sofia answered, forcing her voice to sound as normal as possible. She tried to mask the panic that was clawing at her chest.

Chelsea's voice came through the phone, warm and casual, "Hey, sweetie. How are you feeling?"

Sofia swallowed, trying to push the knot in her throat down. "I'm fine, Mom."

"Good, good. Did you eat anything yet?"

Sofia glanced over at the cereal bowl she had hastily eaten earlier. "Yeah, I had some cereal."

"That's good. I was thinking... do you want me to come home for lunch today? I can pick something up for us," Chelsea offered.

Sofia's stomach flipped at the thought of her mom coming home. No, she didn't want that. But she couldn't say no. Not when her mother was being so... normal. "Sure, if you want," Sofia replied, forcing a smile she couldn't feel.

Chelsea didn't seem to notice anything was off. "Alright, I'll be home soon. I'm just finishing up here. You hang tight."

"Okay," Sofia said quietly, feeling a cold sweat form on her palms. "See you soon."

When the call ended, Sofia sat there for a moment, frozen. Her pulse was racing, her hands shaking as she looked at the journal in her lap. She had to keep it together. She couldn't let her mom suspect anything. But now, with the phone call over, she knew what she had to do. She turned back to the diary, flipping through the pages, her heart pounding in her chest as she continued to read.

April 28, 1998

So as I sit up here writing in my journal, I hear a lot of raging going on—loud banging, and throwing up. What is my brother doing down there? Where are the police? I'm not coming down yet, that's for sure. My brother had to have found the bodies by now, though. I'm starting to get hungry. I thought the police would be here already, but they're not. What in the world is he doing?

Sofia's throat went dry as she read the words. Her heart clenched as she realized what her mom had been writing about. This entry was about the aftermath of the murders—the moment Ash had walked in and found his family dead. It was the moment everything fell apart for him. She could almost hear the chaos in those words—his confusion, his panic, and the desperate measures he must've taken to try and make it all seem like an accident. To hide the truth.

Sofia felt sick to her stomach. How could Ash have done that? How could he have tried to clean up the mess? How could he have been so desperate to protect himself from their mother, knowing the truth? But the truth was clear now—Chelsea had orchestrated it all. She had ensured Ash was never safe.

It sent a chill up Sofia's spine as she sat there, absorbing what she had just learned. Her mom had manipulated Ash, twisted the events, and made sure he would be the one blamed. She had used him like a pawn in her twisted game.

Sofia felt a wave of anger wash over her. How could Chelsea do this? How could she lie to her daughter, to her family, for all these years? What kind of monster could hide behind a mask of normalcy, pretending to be the loving, caring mother, when in reality, she had murdered her own family?

Sofia's breath hitched as she flipped to the next page. She couldn't stop now. The truth had to come out. She had to keep digging. She had to understand everything. For Ash. For Anna. For herself.

But as the words in her mom's journal began to form a clearer picture of that fateful night, Sofia knew one thing for sure—her world had just shattered into a million pieces. And she had no idea how she was ever going to put it all back together.

Thirty Two

Sofia sat in her room, staring at the envelope she had just sealed. Her hand trembled as she placed the final piece of tape over the flap, ensuring that the contents inside would remain untouched until they reached their destination. The diary—her mother's confession—had made her skin crawl from the first page to the last, but now it was her weapon, her way of taking back control. It wasn't enough just to know the truth; she needed someone else to know it too.

She had decided, after days of sleepless nights, that sending the journal anonymously to Stephanie Jacobs was the right thing to do. If anyone could get the truth out, it would be Stephanie. She would take it seriously, make sure it went to the right people. And with that, maybe Ash would finally get the justice he deserved.

The envelope was addressed simply:
Stephanie Jacobs, 442 Oakview Lane, Old Westbury, New York

There was no return address. Sofia knew there would be no turning back once the mailman collected it.

Later that afternoon, Ash met with his lawyer, feeling more uncertain than ever about his future. He had spent the last two decades behind bars for a crime he never committed, all because of his sister's lies. But now, with the new evidence in hand—the journal Sofia had sent—things were about to change. The lawyer looked over the journal's pages, his face growing more serious with each word he read.

"Ash," his lawyer said after a long silence, looking up. "I don't think you remember anything from that night because... well, you simply went to sleep that night, didn't you? You were out cold. You didn't have anything to do with what happened, but they pinned it all on you."

Ash blinked in disbelief. He had always wondered, even in his darkest moments, why he couldn't remember what had happened that night. He had just woken up to chaos, to the brutal aftermath of something he had no part in. His lawyer continued, "This new evidence is going to be a game-changer. It's likely we'll be able to get you released on appeal. You've served time for tampering with a corpse, but with this diary, the case against you might finally be cleared."

Ash ran his hands through his hair, his thoughts racing. Could it really be that easy? Could this small, quiet piece of evidence change everything? His mind spun with the possibilities—he could finally be free, finally clear his name after all these years.

Meanwhile, at home, Chelsea was sitting at her kitchen table, sipping coffee, when there was a knock at the door. She looked up, confused. The knock was firm, insistent, and before she could even stand up to answer it, the door swung open. Two police officers stepped inside.

"Chelsea Reed, you're under arrest for the murders of your parents and sister," one officer announced, his voice sharp and steady.

Chelsea's face froze in shock, her cup of coffee slipping from her hands and splashing onto the floor. "What are you talking about?" she stammered. "I—I don't know what you're talking about. This is a mistake!"

But the officers weren't moved by her protests. They read her her rights and placed her in handcuffs, guiding her out the door. Chelsea's eyes darted frantically around the house, but it was too late. She was going to be taken to the station, and her lies were finally being uncovered.

Sofia stood in the doorway, watching in silence as her mother was escorted into the police cruiser. The weight of what had just happened settled on her chest like a stone. Her heart pounded in her ears, but she didn't dare speak. She couldn't say a word to her mother now. It was over. The secret had been revealed.

Later that evening, as the sun began to set, Sofia sat at the dinner table with her dad. There was no sound between them except the occasional clink of silverware against plates. Neither of them spoke. Neither of them needed to. It felt like the world had shifted in some irrevocable way, and neither of them knew what to say.

For years, they had both lived under Chelsea's shadow, pretending that everything was fine. But now, Sofia couldn't escape the truth. Her mother had killed her family, and now she was gone.

Jonathan Reed ate his food in silence, his face expressionless as the television flickered in the background. The 5 p.m. news anchor's voice broke through the stillness of the room.

"Breaking news tonight: After 26 years, the truth behind the tragic events of April 27th, 1998, has finally come to light. Chelsea Reed, formerly Chelsea Mitchell, has been arrested in connection with the murders of her parents and sister. The case, which had long been suspected to be a case of mistaken identity, now points to Chelsea as the perpetrator. She is accused of framing her brother, Ash Mitchell, for the crime, which led to his conviction and two decades in prison. More updates to follow."

Sofia's father reached for the remote, his fingers stiff, and turned off the TV with a click. Neither of them spoke. They both knew what had just happened, but they didn't need to hear it again.

The room felt cold, filled with an emptiness that words couldn't fill. For the first time in years, the silence wasn't uncomfortable—it was all they had left. The secrets that had once been so carefully buried had now been unearthed, and there was no going back.

Chelsea was gone. The truth was out.

And as the night wore on, Sofia and her father sat together in silence, knowing that their lives had just changed forever.

Thirty Three

Epilogue

The years had passed slowly, but Sofia still carried the weight of her mother's dark secrets. Life without Chelsea was quieter, simpler, but a shadow lingered over everything, casting familiar doubts and unease. Ash had been freed and was rebuilding his life from the ruins of his lost years, often sending Sofia letters half filled with gratitude and half with questions she couldn't answer. Her father, Jonathan, seemed more distant than ever, as though part of him had left with Chelsea the day she was arrested.

One foggy autumn evening, Sofia was packing up her old bedroom in her father's house, preparing for her own move across the country. As she boxed up forgotten pieces of her past, she stumbled upon a loose floorboard in the corner of her mother's bedroom closet. Curiosity tugged at her, and beneath the floorboard, she discovered a folded letter, yellowed and brittle. Her heart thudded as she realized it was from Chelsea.

With trembling hands, Sofia unfolded the paper. The ink was smudged in places, but her mother's familiar, elegant script was unmistakable.

"My dearest Sofia,

If you're reading this, then you've found out a truth I never wanted you to uncover. You think you know the whole story now—that I killed my family and framed your uncle. But the truth is always more complex than it appears. There's more to our family than you understand, and I'm not the only one with secrets.

Before you judge me, know this: I did what I had to. It was survival. But you have questions, I'm sure, and I imagine some of them lead to your father. What did he know? How much did he understand about the events of that night? Did he have a role, even from a distance? Perhaps he didn't—perhaps I'm only planting seeds here, but you should know that trust can be a dangerous thing, especially with those closest to you.

I raised you to be strong, to be careful, to read between the lines. So I leave you with this: Don't trust anyone too easily, even those who smile and assure you of their love. Family has many faces, and some of them hide darker truths.

With all my love,
Mom"

A chill washed over Sofia as she read the words, feeling the calculated malice woven into every line. Chelsea had left her daughter with more than just answers; she'd left her with doubts that would linger, even as she tried to move forward. Sofia's memories began to shift, tainted by her mother's insinuations. Had Chelsea written this letter only to taunt her, to keep her feeling trapped and uncertain? Or was there something she truly didn't know about her father?

As Sofia looked out the window into the darkening twilight, a strange sense of isolation settled in. She understood now that her mother had orchestrated this moment, leaving her with a whisper of doubt, a final twist in a story that was far from over. The secrets of her family would never truly leave her, and with a heavy heart, she realized she might never know whom to trust.

In the silence, only one thing was clear: even now, Chelsea's shadow still loomed over her life, binding her with the secrets they'd all *buried*.

The Secrets We Bury

www.ingramcontent.com/pod-product-compliance
Lightning Source LLC
Chambersburg PA
CBHW031216160726
47992CB00006B/2769